I have often thought that
I am the most clever
woman who ever lived,
and others cannot compare with me.

Cixi, Empress Dowager of China

To Ben—my little emperor

Photographs © 2009: Alamy Images/The Print Collector: 13; Art Resource, NY/HIP: 105; Bridgeman Art Library International Ltd., London/New York: 109 (Fritz Neumann/Private Collection/Archives Charmet), 116 (Private Collection), 93 bottom (Auguste Roubille/Private Collection/The Stapleton Collection), 62 (Edward T.C. Werner/George G. Harrap & Co./Private Collection); Christie's Images Ltd.: 89 top; Corbis Images: 78, 92 top (Spencer Arnold/Hulton-Deutsch Collection), 19, 32, 64 (Bettmann), 56 (Dean Conger), 42 (Hulton-Deutsch Collection), 98, 99 (Philadelphia Museum of Art), 85 (Underwood & Underwood), 75; Everett Collection, Inc./Mary Evans Picture Library: 76; Getty Images: 68 (Eightfish), 40, 90 bottom (Hulton Archive), 88 right (Richard Nowitz), 22 (Keren Su); ImagineChina: 29, 70, 89 center, 90 center; Photoshot: 93 top (AISA/World Illustrated), 93 center, 115 (UPPA); Superstock, Inc./Image Asset Management Ltd.: 90 top; The Art Archive/Picture Desk: 81 (Marc Charmet/Private Collection), 25 (Eileen Tweedy), 89 bottom (Eileen Tweedy/School of Oriental & African Studies); The Granger Collection, New York: 21, 88 left (Rue des Archives), 10, 27, 35, 44, 91 center, 92 center, 101, 119; The Image Works: 39 (Mary Evans Picture Library), 91 bottom (Mary Evans/Ad Lib Studios), 50, 91 top (NMPFT/SSPL), 92 bottom (Roger-Viollet); Wikipedia Commons: 73.

Illustrations by XNR Productions, Inc.: 4, 5, 8, 9
Cover art, page 8 inset by Mark Summers
Chapter art by Raphael Montoliu

Library of Congress Cataloging-in-Publication Data

Price, Sean Stewart.
Cixi : evil empress of China? / Sean Stewart Price.
p. cm. — (A wicked history)
Includes bibliographical references and index.
ISBN-13: 978-0-531-18555-1 (lib. bdg.) 978-0-531-22171-6 (pbk.)
ISBN-10: 0-531-18555-9 (lib. bdg.) 0-531-22171-7 (pbk.)
1. Cixi, Empress dowager of China, 1835-1908. I. Title.
DS763.63.C58P75 2008
951'.035092—dc22
[B]

2008015123

Tod Olson, Series Editor
Marie O'Neill, Art Director
Allicette Torres, Cover Design
SimonSays Design!, Book Design and Production
Pronunciations created with the help of Haihong Shi.
Many thanks to Virginia Moore.

© 2009 Scholastic Inc.

1 2 3 4 5 6 7 8 9 10.R 18 17 16 15 14 13 12 11 10 09   23

A WiCKED HISTORY™

Cixi

Evil Empress of China?

S E A N   S T E W A R T   P R I C E

Franklin Watts®
An Imprint of Scholastic Inc.
New York   Toronto   London   Auckland   Sydney
Mexico City   New Delhi   Hong Kong
Danbury, Connecticut

The World of Empress Cixi

For four decades, Cixi fought a losing battle to keep China's doors closed to foreign influence.

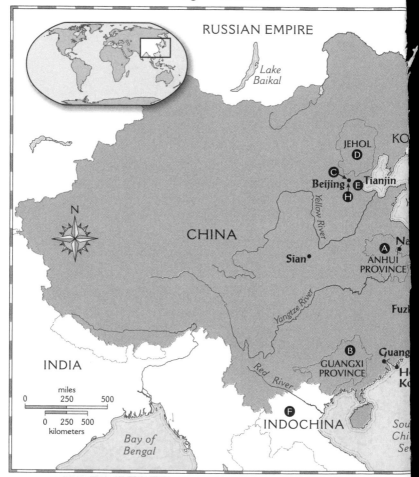

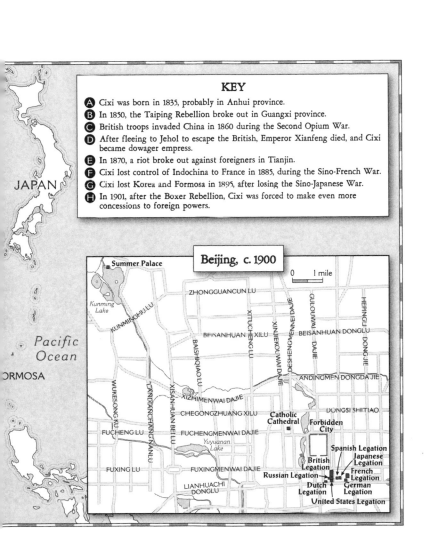

KEY

Ⓐ Cixi was born in 1835, probably in Anhui province.

Ⓑ In 1850, the Taiping Rebellion broke out in Guangxi province.

Ⓒ British troops invaded China in 1860 during the Second Opium War.

Ⓓ After fleeing to Jehol to escape the British, Emperor Xianfeng died, and Cixi became dowager empress.

Ⓔ In 1870, a riot broke out against foreigners in Tianjin.

Ⓕ Cixi lost control of Indochina to France in 1885, during the Sino-French War.

Ⓖ Cixi lost Korea and Formosa in 1895, after losing the Sino-Japanese War.

Ⓗ In 1901, after the Boxer Rebellion, Cixi was forced to make even more concessions to foreign powers.

JAPAN

Pacific
Ocean

ORMOSA

Beijing, c. 1900

Summer Palace

0   1 mile

ZHONGGUANCUN LU

Kunming
Lake

KUNMING-JU LU

BEISANHUAN XILU

XITUCHENGLU

BAISHIQIAO LU

XINJIEKOUWAI DAJIE

DESHENGMENNEI DAJIE

GULOUWAI DAJIE

BEISANHUAN DONGLU

HEPINGLI

DONG JIE

ANDINGMEN DONGDA JIE

WUKESONG KU

LANDIANCHANG NANLU

XISANHUAN BEILU

XIZHIMENWAI DAJIE

CHEGONGZHUANG XILU

Catholic
Cathedral

DONGSI SHITIAO

FUCHENG LU

FUCHENGMENWAI DAJIE

Forbidden
City

Yuyuanan
Lake

FUXING LU

FUXINGMENWAI DAJIE

Spanish Legation

LIANHUACHI
DONGLU

British
Legation

Japanese
Legation

Russian Legation

French
Legation

Dutch
Legation

German
Legation

United States Legation

TABLE OF CONTENTS

A Wicked Web

A look at the allies and enemies of Empress Cixi.

Cixi's Family and Associates

EMPEROR XIANFENG ——— **CIAN**
father of Cixi's son
(known as Niuhuru)
wife of Xianfeng;
empress dowager and
Cixi's co-regent

EMPEROR TONGZHI
(born: Zaichun)
Cixi's son

PRINCE GONG
brother of Xianfeng;
Cixi's co-regent

PRINCE CHUN
brother of Xianfeng;
married to Cixi's sister;
became head of Chinese navy

CIXI,
EMPRESS OF CHINA
(known as **YEHENARA**)

EMPEROR GUANGXU
(born: Zaitian)
Cixi's nephew; selected by
her to become emperor

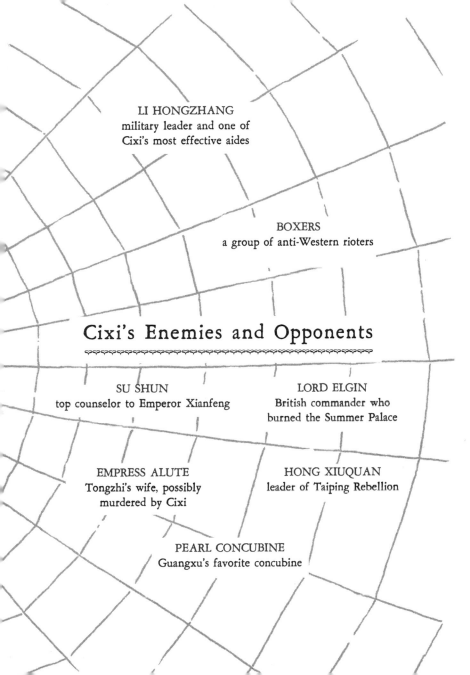

LI HONGZHANG
military leader and one of
Cixi's most effective aides

BOXERS
a group of anti-Western rioters

Cixi's Enemies and Opponents

SU SHUN
top counselor to Emperor Xianfeng

LORD ELGIN
British commander who
burned the Summer Palace

EMPRESS ALUTE
Tongzhi's wife, possibly
murdered by Cixi

HONG XIUQUAN
leader of Taiping Rebellion

PEARL CONCUBINE
Guangxu's favorite concubine

EMPRESS CIXI, 1835–1908

"BURN! BURN! BURN! KILL! KILL! KILL!"

The city of Beijing seemed to have gone mad. Bands of angry rioters stormed through China's capital, armed with swords and spears. The rioters practiced a form of martial arts that earned them the nickname "Boxers" among the terrified foreign residents of the city. The Boxers had one goal in mind: to force all foreigners and Christians out of China. And they were eager to kill anyone who resisted.

Inside the foreign compounds of Beijing, diplomats and their families scrambled to protect themselves from the Boxers. The English, French, Dutch, Americans, Russians, and Japanese turned their offices into a hastily built fort. They made barricades out of expensive tables and chairs. Fine silks were sewn together to make sandbags. People from the Spanish and Belgian embassies, a few blocks away, crept through the streets to take refuge in the fort.

The Germans, on the other side of town, were not so fortunate. Their ambassador tried to reach the Chinese foreign ministry to complain about the attacks. He was shot and killed in the street. The Boxers stormed the German compound before the rest of its staff could escape.

The Chinese capital was under siege. Representatives from the most powerful nations on earth hid in their makeshift fort. Chinese Christians and their European priests took cover in the city's Catholic cathedral, protected by a few French and Italian soldiers. Clouds of smoke spread slowly across the city, mingling with the chant of the Boxers: "Burn! Burn! Burn! Kill! Kill! Kill!"

In the center of Beijing, the sound of the riots drifted over the 26-foot walls of the Forbidden City, home to five centuries of Chinese emperors. No Boxer dared set foot inside the Forbidden City. By law, trespassers there could be put to death.

DURING THE BOXER REBELLION, Empress Cixi backed rebels
who wanted to drive all foreigners out of China.

Still, the Boxers had the support of the Forbidden City's mysterious dowager empress. Her name was Cixi (*tsu shee*), and she had been the power behind China's Qing (*ching*) Dynasty for four decades.

Foreigners knew very little about Cixi. A woman in a country traditionally ruled by men, the empress made her decisions behind the scenes. A silk screen hid her throne from view to make it seem as though she wasn't really in charge. Until just two years earlier, no foreigners had been in her presence without the screen blocking their view.

Like a skilled puppeteer, Cixi pulled the strings for more than 400 million subjects. Nobody doubted that she had set the Boxers loose. It was just her latest gamble in a life full of bold moves. If it worked, China might finally be rid of the hated foreigners.

But failure could mean the end of the Qing Dynasty and centuries of imperial tradition. The foreign powers would see to that. If they didn't, the Chinese people might do it themselves. The Qing Dynasty was widely despised in China—thanks in large part to Cixi. The empress had a reputation for treachery. It was said that she poisoned relatives, murdered servants and enemies, and spent her people's tax money on her personal comfort. She had imprisoned the current emperor for daring to defy her. Supposedly, she fed him from her hand like a dog.

Who was this woman who held the fate of the world's most populous nation in her hands? How did she rise from an obscure family to become one of the most powerful and fearsome women in the world?

Her story begins in a dirt-poor region of China.

PART 1

A Girl in the Forbidden City

CHAPTER 1

Modest Beginnings

A teenager is chosen to JOIN
CHINA'S ROYAL HOUSEHOLD.

THE FUTURE EMPRESS OF CHINA WAS BORN
November 29, 1835, probably in Anhui province. Most
likely, it was not a happy event. Baby girls were
seldom welcome in China. A daughter usually married
as a teenager and became part of her husband's family.
Many girl babies were not even given first names.
Instead, they were designated by birth order—
Number One Girl, Number Two Girl, and so on.
Cixi's birth name has been lost to history, but as a
teenager, she was known as Yehenara.

Yehenara's father was a low-level government official. He brought his family to Beijing when Yehenara was still a child. At the time, the Chinese capital was a chaotic place. A typical street in Beijing was little more than a muddy path. Animals and small children relieved themselves in the dirt. Toothless beggars and street performers competed loudly for the coins of passersby.

WHEN YEHENARA came to Beijing sometime around 1850, the capital (above) was filthy and chaotic. But at its center stood the Forbidden City, a compound of beautiful, secluded palaces.

Fortunetellers, barbers, and soup vendors clogged the way. Scribes prepared letters and other documents for the city's residents. They did a brisk business since few people could read or write.

Yehenara had plenty of entertainment in Beijing. She was fond of puppet plays and shows featuring trained mice. She and her friends played games similar to tag and marbles. By the time she was a young teenager, Yehenara had three younger sisters and one younger brother. As the oldest sister, Yehenara took care of her siblings, carrying them on her back when she ran errands for her mother.

As an adult, Cixi claimed that her early years were unhappy. "I have had a very hard life ever since I was a young girl," she recalled. "I was not a bit happy when with my parents, as I was not the favorite."

But this unloved elder daughter was smart and very pretty. She stood about five feet tall, with lively black eyes and a charming smile. Like most women in China at the time, she wore her black hair in long braids.

YEHENARA WAS an unusually beautiful young woman. At the time, most women of her age had few options in China. Her beauty—and brains—would give her a rare opportunity.

Yehenara had another important asset. She belonged to the Manchu ethnic group. Manchus were outnumbered by the Han majority in China, but the Manchus held all the power. The Manchu-led Qing Dynasty had governed the country since 1644. That placed Yehenara in China's ruling class from birth.

As a beautiful Manchu woman, Yehenara was eligible for a great honor. She could become one of the emperor's concubines. Each emperor in the Qing Dynasty had a wife who served as the empress. He also

A CHINESE EMPEROR with his concubines. This emperor is from the Tang Dynasty, which collapsed in 907. Yehenara was selected to be a concubine more than 900 years later, in 1851.

had concubines. A concubine's main job was to provide male children for the dynasty. If an empress failed to deliver the all-important male heir, the oldest of the concubines' boys would become the next emperor.

When Yehenara was 14, her parents registered her to become a concubine. Competition for the position was fierce. Only a few women out of thousands were selected, and Yehenara had to go through a complicated screening process. She took a series of tests that measured everything from conversational skills to physical defects. The examiners were servants of the empress dowager, the emperor's mother. The empress dowager herself made the final selections.

In 1851, Yehenara was chosen as a concubine. Given the job description, it may not seem like a privilege. But ordinary women in China—even Manchus—faced difficult futures. Yehenara probably would have become a powerless wife in a poor household. Now, at age 16, she was about to leave Beijing's filthy streets and enter a glamorous realm like no other place on earth.

CHINA VS. THE WORLD

AS YEHENARA PREPARED TO TAKE HER PLACE in the emperor's palace, China was being forced into changes that would scar the country for decades.

For four centuries, Chinese leaders had kept the country largely closed to foreign influence. Only one seaport—the city of Guangzhou (*gwahng-jo*)—was allowed to receive foreign ships. The emperors discouraged new ideas and technologies. After all, the Chinese had invented such wonders as gunpowder, the magnetic compass, and the printing press. What could they possibly learn from foreigners, who were known as "barbarians"?

FIRST OPIUM WAR

Western governments often asked for increased trade with China. Chinese leaders refused. In the 1700s, Emperor Qianlong (*chee-en lohng*) told visitors from England: "As [you] can see for [yourselves], we possess all things. I . . . have no use for your country's manufactures."

By the early 1800s, however, Europe turned up the pressure on China. Great Britain, France, and other countries were industrializing quickly. They wanted luxury goods and raw materials from China. They also wanted to sell the products from their factories.

In 1839, the conflict became violent. British traders had been smuggling opium, a powerful drug, into Guangzhou to trade for tea, silk, and pottery. When China tried to crack down on the smuggling, the British launched the First Opium War.

The outdated Chinese military was no match for the British. In 1842, the Chinese were forced to surrender and sign the Treaty of Nanjing. They had to hand over Hong Kong to British control, open five Chinese ports to British traders, and pay a huge fine.

For the Chinese, it was a humiliating defeat— and a painful preview of things to come.

The *Nemesis*, a British ship made partly of iron, destroys wooden Chinese warships during the First Opium War.

CHAPTER 2

In the Forbidden City

YEHENARA LEARNS THE WAYS
of the royal court.

IN 1851, YEHENARA ENTERED THE FORBIDDEN City in a sedan chair carried by servants. "The Great Within," as it was called, was a separate city inside Beijing. Its walls enclosed 250 acres of gracious parks, lakes, and hills. The Forbidden City also held hundreds of beautiful buildings with names like the Hall of Supreme Harmony and Palace of Heavenly Purity. China's ruling elite lived either in the city itself or in the surrounding neighborhood, called the Imperial City.

Yehenara must have been amazed by the sparkling courtyards, giant statues, and white marble staircases of her new home. A couple of weeks earlier, she had been just another teenage girl with braided pigtails. Now she was one of the most important women in all of China. She dressed in stiff silk gowns. Her face was made up

LIFE IN THE FORBIDDEN CITY was controlled by strict ceremony. Yehenara wished to become the emperor's favorite, but opportunities to spend time with him were limited.

with white powder and rouge. Servants stood around her, ready to grant her every wish.

But Yehenara wanted more than just a life of luxury. She wanted a special place at the side of the emperor— and that would not come easily. As a concubine, Yehenara was still just a low-ranking member of the emperor's household. Cixi's competition included the emperor's wife, Empress Niuhuru (*nee-ew hu-lu*), 11 concubines, and two former concubines who had been promoted to the higher rank of consort. Yehenara would have to work to become the emperor's favorite.

The emperor was 20-year-old Xianfeng (*shee-ahn-fung*). He had just taken power after his father's death and had been chosen for the throne over eight brothers. He was interested in literature and politics. But he also loved women, parties, and opium. He left important decisions to his Grand Council of advisers, headed by the Grand Counselor, Su Shun.

Life in the Forbidden City was ruled by ritual and ceremony. The emperor and those around him

YEHENARA WAS TRYING to get the attention of
this man, Emperor Xianfeng. He was the seventh emperor
of the Qing Dynasty. Just 20 years old, he preferred to leave
politics to his advisers.

changed clothes for each new activity. They might wear one outfit for a religious ceremony, another to go hunting, and yet another for relaxing in their private quarters. Each outfit was made from fine silk.

On a typical day, the emperor awoke early in his quarters in the Hall of Mental Cultivation. After breakfast, he met with advisers and took care of government issues. After lunch, he had leisure time. Qing emperors tended to enjoy flying kites, ice-skating, and playing Chinese chess. Supper was served at sunset. Emperor Xianfeng might eat alone or with invited guests. Each meal usually included eight main dishes, four side dishes, two or three hot soups, steamed buns, rice, and cakes. The leftovers were given to court officials and concubines.

When the emperor retired for the night, he put out a small jade plaque. On it was inscribed the name of the woman he wished to see that night. Like all concubines, Yehenara had one goal—to get the emperor to put out her plaque.

Revolt!

Yehenara wins the emperor's affection—AS REBELS TEAR CHINA APART.

YEHENARA SPENT HER EARLY YEARS IN the Forbidden City trying to improve herself. The other concubines were her competition, and she spent little time gossiping with them. Instead, she learned to read and write. She developed a talent for painting and calligraphy, skills that were widely admired at court. She also raised Pekinese dogs, a breed that only members of the royal family were allowed to own.

YEHENARA'S GOAL was to become Emperor
Xianfeng's favorite concubine.

Meanwhile, outside the walls of the Forbidden City, China seemed to be falling apart. A massive earthquake had wrecked farmlands and towns in central China. Harsh weather had brought famine to Beijing. The Qing Dynasty had lost support among the people after its humiliating loss to Great Britain in the First Opium War.

Hungry and tired, poor people around the country were rebelling against their Manchu rulers. And one revolt in particular, the Taiping Rebellion, was threatening to destroy the Qing Dynasty.

The Taiping leader Hong Xiuquan (*hung shee-o chee-en*) was a religious fanatic. He adapted ideas from Christian missionaries who had been coming to China for years. Hong convinced himself that he was Jesus' younger brother and that God wanted him to force all demons out of China. Those demons included the country's Manchu leaders.

Hong preached his message to angry peasants in southern China. By 1851, he had thousands of followers.

Many of them were convinced that Hong could work miracles. It was said he could cut out paper soldiers and then make them come to life.

Hong's real-life army went into battle under the slogan "Plunder the rich to relieve the poor." In January 1851, they defeated the emperor's imperial troops in Guangxi (*gwahng-shee*) province. Eight months later, Hong organized the territory he controlled into a state called the Heavenly Kingdom of Peace. He named himself as its leader.

By 1853, Hong controlled most of south and central China, with the city of Nanjing as his capital. Hong formed a government that ruled about 30 million people. His new regime tossed aside centuries of tradition. New laws banned vices such as opium smoking and gambling. Hong also forbade the use of slaves and abolished private property. His men destroyed traditional religious temples and shrines.

The Taipings struck out at the symbols of Manchu rule. The Manchus insisted that all Chinese men wear

HONG XIUQUAN'S SOLDIERS attack a town during the
Taiping Rebellion. In 1853, they took control of Nanjing,
massacring 30,000 civilians in the city.

a braided ponytail called a queue. The Taipings banned queues and let their hair grow long and wild.

By 1855, the Taipings seemed ready to sweep Emperor Xianfeng and the Manchus from power. They had raised an army of nearly one million well-organized soldiers.

Around the same time, Yehenara scored an important personal victory. On a spring day in 1855, she caught the emperor's attention. She was sewing outdoors among some trees, singing a children's song. He heard a beautiful voice as he walked down a wooded path and demanded to know whom it belonged to. That night, he set out her plaque.

Yehenara bragged that she held great power over Emperor Xianfeng from then on. "When I arrived at Court," she later said, "the late emperor became very much attached to me and would hardly glance at any of the other ladies." She later recalled this time as one of the happiest periods of her life.

When she became pregnant with Xianfeng's child, her happiness seemed complete.

CHAPTER 4

Heir to a Shaky Empire

The birth of Yehenara's son
is overshadowed by
THE SECOND OPIUM WAR.

YEHENARA'S PREGNANCY MADE HER
more than just a concubine. She was now the
emperor's favorite. If she gave birth to a girl, she
would be an important person for life. If she gave
birth to a boy, she would also hold great political
power. Her son would immediately become the heir
to the throne.

Like everything at the emperor's court, the course of a pregnancy was dictated by rigid rules. The mother had to observe good manners. Certain books had to be read aloud to her to educate the child in her womb. She had to avoid any colors or foods that might upset her. Even her pillows had to be arranged perfectly.

On April 27, 1856, the moment Yehenara had been waiting for arrived. She gave birth to a baby boy named Zaichun (*zai-chun*). It was the crowning achievement of her young life. For providing the dynasty with an heir, she was promoted to the rank of consort, making her second in importance only to the Empress Niuhuru.

All across Beijing, people rejoiced. The birth of an heir was considered a good sign for Emperor Xianfeng. Many hoped that his troubles were behind him.

The optimism lasted less than six months.

On October 8, 1856, Emperor Xianfeng stumbled into another conflict with the foreign powers. Chinese troops boarded a cargo ship supposedly flying the

British flag and arrested 12 crew members. The sailors were charged with smuggling illegal goods.

The British, who were looking for an excuse to go to war, claimed they were outraged by the arrests. Since the end of the First Opium War, the British had been pressing for more privileges from China. They wanted the Chinese to legalize the opium trade, welcome foreign diplomats in Beijing, and allow foreigners to travel throughout China.

CHINESE TROOPS ARREST British sailors for smuggling. This incident provoked the Second Opium War.

In 1857, the Second Opium War began. This time the British were joined by the French, who also wanted to trade in China. Foreign troops occupied Guangzhou and invaded two Chinese provinces. Again, the Chinese soldiers proved no match for the Europeans. The British commander, Lord Elgin, scorned the Chinese military. "Twenty-four determined men with revolvers and a sufficient number of cartridges might walk through China from one end to another," he said.

MEMBERS OF A MILITIA from the Chinese countryside during the Second Opium War. Their clubs and shields were useless against European rifles.

Emperor Xianfeng's advisers had little choice but to negotiate a new treaty, known as the Treaty of Tianjin. They agreed to open 11 more ports to foreign trade. They also allowed foreign ships to travel on some Chinese rivers. Foreigners were given the right to travel anywhere in China.

However, as soon as the agreement was concluded, Emperor Xianfeng's advisers convinced him he had made a mistake. He refused to honor the treaty.

By June 1859, England and France grew tired of waiting for the emperor to approve the treaty. They ordered troops to escort representatives to their new embassies in Beijing.

The Chinese decided to resist. In a fierce battle near Tianjin, Chinese cannons sank four foreign gunboats. And the following year, the emperor ordered a British negotiator to be arrested and tortured. The war would continue.

THE EVILS OF OPIUM

IN THE EARLY 1800s, OPIUM WAS LEGAL IN Europe and the United States. In liquid form, it was used for everything from curing headaches to quieting crying babies.

However, the dangers of the drug were well known. "It wastes the flesh and blood until the skin hangs down in bags and their bones are as naked as billets of wood," one observer wrote. "When the smoker has pawned everything in his possession [to keep buying the drug], he will pawn his wife and sell his daughters."

In China, the emperor outlawed the opium trade in 1796. Still, Britain continued to bring the drug into the country, and opium addiction became a widespread problem. Even Emperor Xianfeng was most likely an addict.

The Chinese fought two hopeless wars to keep opium out of their country.

CHINESE MEN in an opium den in around 1900.

CHAPTER 5

Up in Flames

China's royal treasures are left to the
MERCY OF THE "BARBARIANS."

ON AUGUST 19, 1860, PANIC ROCKED
China's royal household. British and French forces
were bearing down on Beijing. Yehenara followed
the progress of the war from the Summer Palace—a
beautiful complex of fountains, gardens, and palaces
outside Beijing. She had lived there for the previous
three years, gardening or sitting by the palace lake.
The imperial boat, rowed by 24 male servants
called eunuchs, gave her a place to cool off from the
summer heat.

With the foreign armies closing in, Yehenara rushed around frantically, trying to save what she could. Hundreds of wagons were filled with clothes and artwork. But most of the treasures had to be left behind. The important thing was to head north to safety.

Yehenara, the emperor, and thousands of refugees left in a grand procession. For ten days, they trekked northward toward Jehol (*juh-hul*), the emperor's hunting retreat. Yehenara rode on a giant orange sedan chair

THE ROYAL FAMILY RELAXES at the Summer Palace.
Yehenara was forced to flee from this luxurious complex when
the British and French invaded in 1860.

carried on the shoulders of servants. The slapping of their sandals mixed with the sound of women weeping as they left their homes behind.

Finally, the refugees reached the safety of Jehol. The emperor gathered his advisers to figure out how to save the Qing Dynasty. He had left his brother, Prince Gong, behind to negotiate with the foreigners.

The news from Prince Gong was not good. A combined British and French force had reached the abandoned Summer Palace at dawn on October 7. Inside, they found centuries' worth of treasures. The amazed invaders spoke in whispers as they walked through the many pavilions.

Then the looting began. Soldiers stole whatever they could pick up and shot or smashed what they couldn't. They carried away statues, porcelain, jade, jewelry, furs, furniture, and rolls of silk.

After the palaces had been stripped of their treasures, the British commander, Lord Elgin, decided to send a message that would humble the Chinese. He ordered the Summer Palace burned. On October 18, 1860, its glorious buildings were torched.

Two days after the destruction of the Summer Palace, Prince Gong gave in to the demands of the foreigners. These demands were even worse than the Treaty of Tianjin. China had to pay huge sums of money to the foreign powers. The sale of opium became legal, and ten more ports were opened for trade. The foreign powers were allowed to set up offices for diplomats in Beijing. Christian missionaries were given the legal right to preach in China.

Back in Jehol, Emperor Xianfeng was overwhelmed by this defeat. Years of drug use and disease had weakened him. Now his spirit was crushed. Rumors buzzed through the court that either Yehenara or advisers such as Su Shun were poisoning him. Xianfeng kept to his room in the Hall of Refreshing Mists and Waves. He was dying.

CHAPTER 6

Death of an Emperor

Yehenara saves herself and TAKES POWER AS EMPRESS CIXI.

XIANFENG'S DECLINE PRESENTED A GREAT opportunity for Yehenara. Her five-year-old son Zaichun would soon become emperor. By tradition, she would become regent, or decision-maker, for the young emperor. She would share that duty with Empress Niuhuru.

But Yehenara's position was shaky—not to mention dangerous. She had fierce competition from Grand

Chancellor Su Shun, who was determined to become the regent. Su Shun did not believe women should occupy positions of power. He would never agree to share power with Yehenara and Niuhuru. If he won the coming power struggle, he might look for an excuse to have the two women executed.

For the moment, Su Shun and his followers were in control. They kept the dying emperor isolated. They allowed only a few people to see him and closely supervised all visits. They planned to let Xianfeng die and then claim that the emperor had said that they should be the regents.

Yehenara made her move on August 22, 1861. She appeared at the emperor's bedroom door with her five-year-old son. A small group of officials crowded around Xianfeng's deathbed. Yehenara took the boy to the emperor's side and demanded: "What is to be done about your successor to the throne?"

Xianfeng was weak and pale. He did not answer at first. Desperate, Yehenara said, "Here is your son!"

With that, Xianfeng opened his eyes. "Of course," he whispered, "he will succeed to the throne. His mothers will be his regents."

Xianfeng died minutes later.

Su Shun had been outsmarted. There were too many witnesses for him to deny the emperor's deathbed wish. The next morning, Su was forced to announce to the court that Yehenara and the Empress Niuhuru would rule as regents. They were both promoted to the rank of empress dowager. Yehenara became known as Cixi, Empress of the West. Niuhuru took the name Cian (*tsu-en*), Empress of the East. Their titles referred to the locations of their houses in the Forbidden City.

But Su Shun refused to give up power without a fight. He was determined to get Cixi and Cian under his control. He even tried to cut off their food supply to starve them into submission.

Cixi was ready for Su Shun's challenge. She and Cian made a secret deal with the dead emperor's brother,

PRINCE GONG, Cixi's brother-in-law, formed an alliance with Cixi and the Empress Cian to take control of the country after Emperor Xianfeng's death.

Prince Gong. The prince convinced top government and military officials in Beijing to support the two empresses. In return, the empresses agreed to share power with him.

On November 1, Cixi accompanied the emperor's body back to the Forbidden City, guarded by loyal troops. With the military on his side, Prince Gong had Su Shun and his followers arrested. Su Shun was sentenced to "death by a thousand cuts." But the empresses forbade this torture. Instead, he was beheaded.

A new era had begun.

PART 2

Behind the Silk Curtain

CHAPTER 7

Back to Beijing

Cixi tries to RESTORE ORDER TO THE EMPIRE.

WHEN CIXI AND THE IMPERIAL COURT returned to Beijing late in 1861, they inspected the damage from the war. The foreign powers had not damaged the Forbidden City. But the Summer Palace was a burned-out shell. Several centuries' worth of priceless artwork had been stolen and sent overseas into the homes of wealthy English lords.

The Qing Dynasty had been humiliated, and Cixi went to work to restore its pride. She renamed her son Tongzhi (*tung-juh*), which means "return to order and joint rule." The name symbolized the joint rule of Tongzhi's three regents—Cixi, Cian, and Prince Gong.

Cian had no interest in politics and left Cixi and Prince Gong to dominate the partnership. Prince Gong would serve as the young emperor's top adviser and head of the Grand Council, but Cixi had to approve Gong's decisions.

Empress Cixi was dedicated to the business of government. Every morning, a eunuch brought her a stack of small gold boxes. Each box contained a report from a government adviser or the governor of a province. She opened the reports with an ivory knife, read them, and then handed them to Tongzhi.

When Tongzhi met with advisers and officials, the young emperor sat on his own throne. Cixi and Cian sat behind him, masked by a translucent silk curtain. The curtain was meant to give the idea that the empresses stayed in the background. It was Prince Gong who spoke directly with government advisers and other officials.

From behind the curtain, however, Cixi took charge of the country. Her first goal was to end the Taiping Rebellion once and for all.

By early 1863, the Chinese people were growing tired of the rebels and their leader, Hong. The civil war had devastated an area as big as France and Germany combined. The rebels had given up their commitment to the poor in favor of killing and looting. "Now when the

IN THE FORBIDDEN CITY, the throne room was in the Hall of Mental Cultivation. Here, Cixi stayed hidden behind a silk screen—and controlled the country.

people hear of the arrival of the rebels, pain and regret pierce their hearts," one imperial leader reported. "Men as well as women flee, and kitchen fires no longer burn."

Under Xianfeng and Su Shun, the imperial army had failed to crush the rebellion. Cixi and Prince Gong tried to improve the army. They promoted skilled commanders. These commanders were ordered to recruit better soldiers and treat them well. One of these commanders, Li Hongzhang (*lee hung-jahng*), would become Cixi's close ally for decades to come.

Li used whatever tactics were necessary to strike at the rebels. Desperate for more troops, he paid an American adventurer to bring in a private army of foreign soldiers. The grandly named "Ever Victorious Army" brought artillery and steam-driven gunboats into battle and showed the Chinese how to fight a modern war.

Li was ruthless in battle. Under orders from Cixi and Gong, he took very few prisoners. The Qing leaders wanted none of Hong's followers left alive to start new rebellions. One of Li's generals convinced a Taiping force to surrender after promising its leaders safety. But Li promptly had the rebel leaders executed.

The Taiping generals made their last stand at Nanjing on July 19, 1864. Imperial troops stormed the city. For three days, they battled the rebels from street to street. The death toll was brutal. "Not one of the 100,000 rebels in Nanjing surrendered themselves when the city was taken," an imperial commander reported. "But in many cases [they] gathered together and burned themselves and passed away without repentance."

After nearly 15 years, the Taiping Rebellion was over. Nearly 20 million people had been killed by starvation or bloodshed during the revolt. The rebel leader, Hong, died a month before the final battle. His body was dug up and burned. The ashes were scattered to make sure his spirit would have no final resting place.

CHAPTER 8

Self-Strengthening

Gong tries to modernize China—and
EMPRESS CIXI MAKES HIM
PAY FOR IT.

THE DEFEAT OF THE TAIPING REBELLION
came as a big relief to Cixi. But it did nothing to solve
another serious problem. China's loss in the Second
Opium War had made it clear that the nation was a
second-rate power in the modern world.

Now, the victors were forcing change on China.
Diplomats from England, France, Russia, and the
United States set up their embassies in Beijing. Christian
missionaries arrived to build churches and win Chinese

followers. Foreign ships sailed into the new treaty ports, loaded with goods from Europe.

The presence of the foreigners set off a big debate inside the Forbidden City. Should the Chinese reject the ways of the foreigners, or try to learn from the so-called "barbarians"?

Prince Gong took the most flexible approach. Under his guidance, China began its so-called "Self-Strengthening Movement." The idea was to use Western ideas and technology to help China compete with the rest of the world.

Meanwhile, Li Hongzhang and other military officials began to modernize China's army. Li built factories to produce rifles and Western-style warships. Prince Gong also helped start a school in Beijing staffed with foreign teachers. Students there could study astronomy, math, and foreign languages such as English, French, and Russian.

In April 1865, however, Cixi lashed out at Prince Gong and his reforms. She had Tongzhi, who was just nine years old, issue a decree. "Prince Gong ... exploiting my youthfulness often . . . tried to dominate me," the decree read. "He tried to create misunderstandings between me and the . . . dowagers. Also, during the daily audience, Prince Gong has always been haughty and behaves insincerely."

Cixi stripped Prince Gong of most of his government positions. Still, Gong continued to push his reforms. Cixi went along with many of them. But she was deeply attached to the old ways and suspicious of foreign influence. Years later, she allowed reformers to send groups of Chinese boys to study in the United States. When they came back thinking like Westerners, she canceled the program. In another case, she opposed the building of a railway in Beijing for fear it would "disturb the Emperor's tombs." Li Hongzhang convinced her to allow construction, but she insisted he use horses to pull the cars.

LAND OF CONFUCIUS

THE PEOPLE OF CHINA HAD PRIZED stability and tradition over innovation since the days of Confucius. He was a philosopher from the fifth century B.C. Confucius urged people to obey their elders and respect their ancestors. He believed that women should take leadership roles only within the family. More than 2,300 years after his death, his teachings were still the basis for China's government.

China's government officials, known as *mandarins*, had to pass a series of grueling exams based on Confucian ideas. Passing these tests required years of study at special schools. Only about five percent of all test takers became mandarins. These mandarins were granted respect—and usually devoted their lives to protecting China's Confucian tradition.

Confucius,
551—479 B.C.

CHAPTER 9

Massacre in Tianjin

Missionaries cause TURMOIL THROUGHOUT CHINA.

CIXI DID NOT HAVE TO LOOK HARD TO find the most obvious sign of foreign influence in China—Christian missionaries. By 1870, priests and ministers had been preaching legally in China for a decade. In many cities, their church steeples competed for space with traditional shrines. Chinese converts to Christianity went to church on Sunday with Bibles in their hands and crosses around their necks.

CHINESE CHRISTIANS GATHER in the 1880s. Missionaries
had been coming to China for centuries. They brought new ideas
about medicine and education. They were often criticized for
interfering with the Chinese way of life.

Cixi, like many Chinese, scorned the converts.
"These Chinese Christians are the worst people in
China," she said. "They rob the poor country people
of their land and property, and the missionaries always
protect them—to get a share themselves."

Christian missionaries were in fact protected from
many Chinese laws by the treaties that followed the
Second Opium War. And the missionaries, in turn,

often protected their converts. As a result, many Chinese criminals suddenly became Christians.

Cixi, who was a lifelong Buddhist, found Christian attitudes about religion baffling. China had three main spiritual traditions—Buddhism, Taoism, and Confucianism. Each of these belief systems had existed side-by-side for centuries. Many of their rituals mixed easily with each other and with traditional ancestor worship.

But many of the missionaries showed little respect for other religious beliefs. Priests ordered Chinese converts to stop worshipping at traditional shrines or ancestral tombs.

Some missionaries made matters worse by demanding honors usually reserved for high-ranking Chinese officials. On the streets of Beijing and other cities, one could find Catholic bishops riding in sedan chairs carried by Chinese Christians. A drummer would walk ahead of them, and everyone on the street had to stop and show respect.

As the missionaries pushed deeper into China, the anger against them turned into violence. Anti-Christian attacks became common. Most of the attacks were small fights involving a few individuals. But in the summer of 1870, a full-fledged riot broke out in the city of Tianjin.

At the center of the riot was an orphanage run by French nuns. The orphanage paid people to bring in children. Many Chinese believed—rightly—that the practice encouraged kidnappers to steal children and sell them to the orphanage. Wild rumors spread about the nuns. People accused them of plucking out babies' eyes for use in magic potions.

On June 21, 1870, an angry crowd gathered around the orphanage. A French diplomat armed himself with pistols and stormed across town to complain to a local government official. A hostile mob followed. When the Chinese official refused to do anything, the diplomat pulled out a gun and fired. He missed the official and hit a bystander.

The mob exploded in anger. They charged through the city, looking for foreigners and Christians. They tortured and murdered the French diplomat. Two priests, ten nuns, three Russians, another Frenchman, and dozens of Chinese Christians were also killed in the riot.

The massacre outraged the foreign powers. The French sent gunboats to Tianjin and demanded that the guilty be punished.

Cixi and her advisers were forced to respond. They beheaded 16 men and apologized for the incident. They also tried to create new laws to control the missionaries. The foreign powers refused to discuss the matter.

BAD FENG SHUI

THE CHINESE BELIEVED THAT CONSTRUCTING a home or building affected the spirit world. This "earth magic" was called Feng Shui (*fung schway*). According to the rules of Feng Shui, a door in the wrong place might welcome demons. A wall in the wrong place might keep good spirits out. No building or road in China was built without first consulting an expert in Feng Shui.

Christian missionaries generally considered Feng Shui to be superstitious nonsense. They made their churches tall and impressive-looking and built them wherever they pleased. Foreigners also laid railroad tracks and telegraph lines with no regard for the surroundings. Many Chinese people felt that these projects destroyed the balance and harmony of their world.

THIS TEMPLE was built according to the rules of Feng Shui.

CHAPTER 10

Like Father, Like Son

Emperor Tongzhi turns out to be CORRUPT—JUST LIKE HIS FATHER.

ON JUNE 29, 1873, THE EMPEROR TONGZHI sat cross-legged on a raised platform. Before him stood a small crowd of foreign diplomats. It was the first time in eight decades that a Chinese emperor had met with foreigners.

The diplomats bowed low in respect to Tongzhi. But they did not *kowtow*, the traditional Chinese

TONGZHI, CIXI'S SON and the Qing Dynasty's eighth emperor. Tongzhi was an indifferent leader who barely learned to read. He died young, and people whispered that his mother had murdered him.

greeting that required visitors to touch their foreheads to the floor. For the foreign powers, the meeting was a sign that relations were improving with China. But for Cixi and others in China, it was just one more humiliation.

Cixi had by this time supposedly retired as regent. Her son was 17. He was married now, to the Empress Alute. He had been granted full powers as emperor the year before. But in reality, Cixi had never given up control over China. Tongzhi was too much his father's son to rule on his own.

Tongzhi never took much of an interest in education or the business of government. Cixi's teachers made him study many hours every day, yet at 16, he could barely read. Instead, he liked to spend his time with women and exploring Beijing's opium dens.

Like his father before him, Tongzhi became a scandal. Rumors hummed through Beijing that his mother had deliberately corrupted him to make him easier to manage. Cixi herself was scornful of her son's behavior. "I was lucky in giving birth to a son," she said much later. "But after that I had very bad luck."

In 1874, after ruling officially for just two years, the emperor became ill. The imperial family announced that he had smallpox. Many suspected that Cixi poisoned him by passing along a handkerchief contaminated with the disease, but the charge was never proven. He died on January 12, 1875.

The death of Tongzhi should have ended Cixi's reign in China. The royal family was large, and many members stood in line to take the throne.

But as Tongzhi lay dying, Cixi sent a secret message to Li Hongzhang. She ordered him to quietly march a battalion of soldiers to Beijing. In the dead of night, Li's men sneaked into the Forbidden City. Each man carried a wooden bit in his mouth to keep him from talking.

By morning, Cixi had 4,000 loyal soldiers stationed in the heart of the Forbidden City. Cixi's eunuchs pointed out palace guards who might be disloyal. Those men were quickly arrested, tied up, and sent off to prison.

With the Forbidden City under control, Cixi rode out with Empress Dowager Cian in covered sedan chairs. Their destination was the home of Cixi's sister. She was married to Prince Chun, a brother of Prince Gong and Xianfeng. They had a four-year-old son named Zaitian (*zai ti-yen*). Cixi intended to make her little nephew the next emperor.

WAS CIXI A POISONER?

CIXI HAD MANY ENEMIES WITHIN THE royal court. After the emperor died, their hopes for overthrowing her depended on Tongzhi's wife, the Empress Alute. She was said to be pregnant. If the child was a boy, he would automatically become the new emperor, and Cixi would no longer be regent.

Conveniently for Cixi, Alute died just months after her husband. The death looked like a suicide, and her pregnancy was never confirmed. But Cixi's enemies were convinced that Cixi had poisoned her daughter-in-law.

There is no clear evidence of Cixi's guilt. Alute's father continued to work as a loyal official for Cixi for 25 years after his daughter's death, implying that he trusted Cixi. Then again, self-interest may have won out over family loyalties. The man might simply have been scared of following his daughter to the grave.

THE EMPRESS ALUTE: Did Cixi murder her?

CHAPTER 11

"Glorious Succession"

Cixi selects a new emperor—and TAKES CONTROL AGAIN.

SHORTLY AFTER TONGZHI'S DEATH, members of the Manchu royal family held a tense meeting to decide who would be the next emperor. Cixi waited until the arguments had run their course. Then she announced that she and Empress Dowager Cian would adopt her nephew Zaitian and that he would take the throne. "Here is your emperor!" she declared.

With Li's soldiers in control of the Forbidden City, there was little anyone could do. All debate stopped. The new emperor, now called Guangxu (*gwahng-shoo*), had been chosen.

Back in charge, Cixi stumbled into a new era of turmoil, unable and unwilling to adjust to the challenges arriving from the West. Foreigners were making their way to China in ever larger numbers. They brought with them modern ideas and modern technology. Steamships sailed up and down Chinese rivers, carrying goods from town to town. Railroads and telegraph lines began to

THE EMPEROR GUANGXU on horseback. Cixi's nephew was just four years old when Cixi chose him to take the throne.

connect large cities. Banks funded Chinese merchants who made fortunes in tea and shipping. Missionary schools taught Western ideas about democracy.

With Cixi and other conservatives in power, the Chinese government failed to adapt. Complicated traditions made it difficult to get any kind of change approved. Local officials had to refer all important

CIXI COULD NOT STOP Europe's interference in China. Westerners began to build railroads and telegraph lines to open up the country for trade.

decisions to superiors in Beijing. These superiors were always understaffed. One mandarin might oversee the affairs of 250,000 people. Well-placed bribes were needed to get anything done. Cixi's chief eunuch was whispered to be a millionaire many times over thanks to "the squeeze" he put on people seeking to influence Cixi. The empress dowager herself often took fees to see people.

What's more, the gap between rich and poor widened. As trade with the foreign powers grew, a few Chinese merchants grew fabulously wealthy. Most other Chinese people were living with very little. Millions fled to the United States or South America to start new lives. Those who stayed at home grew more bitter toward both the Manchus and the foreigners.

In 1877, natural disaster added to the discontent. Famine struck in northern China. Several rainless summers had left fields barren and people desperate for food. Hunger and disease killed at least ten million. The government was nearly useless in its relief efforts. Sacks of grain rotted on riverbanks because local officials could not figure out how to transport them inland. "In every village a brooding silence told of the stupefied misery of those who, still living, were only awaiting death," one foreign observer wrote. According to some witnesses, meat markets openly sold human flesh.

The suffering took an enormous toll. But for the Chinese people, there were more disasters to come.

THESE PEASANTS from the Chinese countryside were living in a stone hut. A few of Cixi's people became rich, but millions suffered terribly.

࿐࿐࿐࿐࿐࿐࿐࿐࿐࿐࿐࿐

CHAPTER 12

War Comes Again

Cixi uses another military disaster to
GET RID OF HER
LAST PARTNER IN POWER.

In APRIL OF 1881, CIXI'S PARTNER, THE
Empress Dowager Cian, died suddenly. She was only
45 years old and seemingly in good health. People
immediately began whispering that Cixi had poisoned
yet another rival—despite the fact that Cian had
never been a threat to Cixi's authority.

Around the time of Cian's death, Cixi faced another
challenge from a European power. Since the mid-
1800s, France had been trying to take over Indochina,

a region on China's southern border that the Chinese considered theirs. Like Great Britain and other Western powers, France wanted colonies that could provide raw materials for its factories and markets for the goods they produced.

In 1882, French troops arrived in the Red River Valley, just south of China. Cixi sent Li Hongzhang to negotiate. Li realized that China's army and navy would never stand a chance against France's modern military. He urged Cixi to make a deal with the French, even if she had to give up territory. Prince Gong, however, insisted that China stand up to the foreigners, even if that meant going to war.

In 1883, Gong got his way, and Chinese troops moved into Indochina. The Chinese held their own along the Red River. But on August 23, 1884, French warships surprised the outdated Chinese navy at the port of Fuzhou. Within 30 minutes, the French sank or captured China's entire fleet. Dead Chinese sailors washed up on beaches for days. "It was hardly possible to cross the river anywhere without seeing some of these dreadful reminders of French treachery and brutality," one Englishman wrote.

The ground war dragged on for another year until Li finally negotiated a settlement. China gave up its claim to Indochina, and the Qing Dynasty was left reeling from another humiliation.

Cixi used this disgrace to get rid of her opposition on the Grand Council. She demoted Gong and several

FRENCH WARSHIPS (with the striped flags) launch a surprise attack on the port of Fuzhou. Chinese ships were battered to pieces while still at anchor. As a result, China lost Indochina to France.

of his allies for supporting the war. In Gong's place, she elevated Prince Chun, the father of the young Emperor Guangxu. Prince Chun became head of the navy.

Empress Cixi stood at the height of her power. But to the Chinese people, the future did not look bright. Traditional beliefs held that Chinese emperors ruled with the approval of Heaven. Natural disasters and political defeats were seen as signs from the gods. If an emperor presided over enough disasters, it was thought that he had lost the approval of Heaven. To many Chinese, it seemed as though Guangxu and Cixi had reached that point. The empress was captain of a sinking ship.

CHAPTER 13

The Marble Boat

The empress dowager BUILDS HER
RETIREMENT HOME.

As THE CHINESE PEOPLE ENDURED
famine, poverty, and the upheaval brought by the
foreign powers, Cixi lived in isolation from it
all. She left the Forbidden City only to visit the
tombs of her ancestors. On these rare occasions, all
streets along the route were closed to traffic.
Homeowners had to shut their doors and draw
curtains on windows. People were ordered off the
street upon pain of death until Cixi's sedan chair
had passed.

Inside the Forbidden City, Cixi lived in a world of luxury. Her living quarters had high pink walls and beautifully tended courtyards full of cherry, peach, and plum trees. Songbirds sang sweetly in their cages. Furniture was carved from fine dark wood. Most of her sheets, pillows, furniture, and curtains were either yellow, the official color of the emperor, or blue.

Cixi had a massive collection of jewelry and clothing. By the time she died, the empress dowager had more than 3,000 ebony boxes full of pins, bracelets, and necklaces. She changed clothes often in order to show off her jewels and her wardrobe. Preparing for an audience often took hours.

Some of Cixi's treasured possessions were gifts from subjects who were eager to win her favor. Many of her possessions, however, were paid for by taxing the people of China. That money could have been spent on famine victims or the outdated Chinese military. Instead it funded the favorite projects of the crumbling Qing Dynasty.

One project in particular nearly drained the Chinese treasury. In the mid 1870s, Cixi had ordered the burned-out Summer Palace to be rebuilt. The restoration cost millions of dollars in today's money. Huge sums were taken from the navy to build the "Marble Boat," a building that was shaped like a boat. Meanwhile, the real boats of China's fleet remained rundown and helpless against Europe's modern warships.

In 1887, while work on the Summer Palace was in full swing, another natural disaster struck. Weeks of relentless rainfall caused the Yellow River to overflow its banks. The river flooded an area roughly

ON CIXI'S ORDERS, money that should have been spent replacing China's outdated warships was used to restore the Summer Palace's "Marble Boat."

the size of Louisiana. The initial flooding killed hundreds of thousands. Polluted floodwater spread disease throughout the countryside, and the death toll eventually reached about two million. It was history's most destructive flood.

Once again, the survivors received almost no help from the government. As with previous disasters, many people blamed the Manchus for bringing bad fortune on China. They also blamed the foreigners, whose railways and mines were thought to be scarring the earth and upsetting the balance of nature.

Cixi's regency over Emperor Guangxu should have ended the same year as the flood, when the emperor turned 15. But she decided that Guangxu was not yet ready to rule. He was always sickly and uncertain.

The emperor feared his aunt—and for good reason. Cixi had a reputation for brutality. She was famously thin-skinned and often imagined insults. She punished disrespectful eunuchs by gouging them with her six-inch fingernails. Those who seriously displeased her could face beatings. Anyone she suspected of outright disloyalty would pay with their lives.

Cixi, in turn, saw Guangxu as a weakling. Their relations became even more strained when Cixi chose Guangxu's empress. Guangxu hated the woman and she hated him back. Cixi had more success in selecting concubines. One of the women, the Pearl Concubine, became Guangxu's favorite.

In March 1889, Cixi again announced her retirement as regent, leaving Guangxu to rule as emperor. At 54, she went to live at the rebuilt Summer Palace. This was her "haven of rest after eighteen years of regency," she said. Here, she would grow flowers, raise dogs, and grow old.

But for Cixi, retirement merely meant giving up day-to-day duties. She took with her the great seals, which were needed to approve imperial orders. She also reserved the right to review all state documents and to hire and fire officials.

Cixi still held tremendous power. It would not be long before she used it.

Empress Cixi in Pictures

A MANCHU GIRL

Yehenara was the daughter of a minor
government official. Her family was
part of the Manchu ethnic group,
which ruled over China's Han majority.

THE FORBIDDEN CITY

In 1851, Yehenara was chosen to become one of Emperor
Xianfeng's concubines. She was happy to escape the filthy
streets of Beijing for the secretive luxury of the Forbidden City.

BRAINS AND BEAUTY

As this painting shows, Yehenara was a talented artist. It was her combination of beauty, intelligence, and creativity that won her the role of concubine.

IMMATURE EMPEROR

Just 20 years old, Xianfeng was uninterested in the challenges of politics. He preferred parties, opium, and women.

CHINA TORN IN TWO

Taiping rebels invade the city of Nanjing. Their leader, Hong Xiuquan, believed he was destined to overthrow the Manchu "demons." By 1853, Hong ruled over more than 30 million people.

A HOPELESS FIGHT

This Chinese artwork shows a battle during the Second Opium War, which began in 1857. The British and French riflemen easily defeated the Chinese military.

HEIR TO THE THRONE

In 1856, Yehenara gave birth to Zaichun. As the only son of Emperor Xianfeng, he would be the heir to the throne. His birth raised Yehenara's status.

THE SUMMER PALACE

Yehenara and other members of the royal family were forced to flee this luxurious retreat when British and French troops invaded nearby Beijing.

PRINCELY REFORMER

After Emperor Xianfeng died, his brother Prince Gong helped Yehenara gain power. Yehenara's young son was declared emperor. But, behind the scenes, Gong and Yehenara—now called Cixi— took control.

RUTHLESS GENERAL

Li Hongzhang (right) poses with U.S. President Ulysses S. Grant. Li improved the Chinese military but never defeated a European power.

PERSECUTION OF CHRISTIANS

Crowds prepare for the execution of a Christian woman. Cixi believed that Christian missionaries meant to sabotage China.

THE PEOPLE SUFFER

Famines and floods killed millions of Chinese during Cixi's reign. To many Chinese, these tragedies were signs that the gods no longer approved of the Qing Dynasty.

ANOTHER HUMILIATION

The *Kow-Shing*, a Chinese transport ship, was sunk by the Japanese in 1894.

EMPEROR GUANGXU

After Cixi's son died, she chose her nephew to become emperor. When Guangxu tried to make reforms to modernize China, Cixi humiliated him.

BOXER REBELLION

Starting in 1898, Chinese rebels—called Boxers—attacked foreigners whom they believed were corrupting China. Cixi supported these rebels.

LEFT IN RUINS

The United States, Japan, and six European nations invaded China to crush the Boxers. They left much of the capital in ruins.

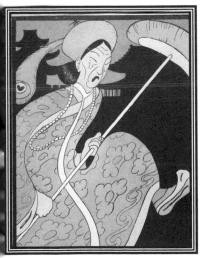

SCORNED EMPRESS

A wailing Cixi stamps her feet in this French cartoon. In 1901, China was forced to sign a humiliating peace treaty, and Cixi was left with very little power.

PART 3

The Last Empress

CHAPTER 14

One Hundred Days

Guangxu tries to remake the
empire—AND HIS AUNT COMES
OUT OF RETIREMENT.

THE YEAR 1894 WAS SUPPOSED TO BE A
year of celebration for Cixi. She was turning 60,
and massive celebrations were planned. New arches
spanned the road to the Summer Palace. All public
officials planned to offer up to 25 percent of their
annual pay as a giant birthday gift.

But the festivities were cut short when yet another
foreign power tried to carve away a piece of the Chinese
empire. For centuries, Chinese emperors had controlled

the Korean peninsula, which lay on the east coast of China, just 100 miles from Japan. In July, the Japanese decided it was time to push the Chinese out. About 4,500 Japanese troops invaded the peninsula, and the two powers went to war.

The Chinese were hopelessly outfought at sea and on land. In September 1894, China's main naval fleet was shot to pieces. Chinese battleships had only 25 rounds of ammunition per gun. On the ground, well-equipped Japanese troops forced the Chinese out of Korea and then pressed on into China.

In April 1895, the Chinese were forced to sign another humiliating treaty. Emperor Guangxu gave up Korea, as well as Formosa (present-day Taiwan). He also agreed to open four ports to Japanese trading ships and pay the victors a fortune.

The defeat infuriated the Chinese. They could not believe they had lost to the Japanese. Just 50 years earlier, Japan had been as isolated as China. And like China, the Japanese had been forced by the Western

JAPANESE ARTWORK showing a victory in the war to take Korea. Chinese sailors dive into the sea from their burning ships.

powers to open their doors to trade. But once they did, Japan reacted much differently than China. The Japanese eagerly adopted Western telegraphs, weapons, and military tactics. Japan modernized—while preserving its culture and keeping its borders secure.

For the modernizers in China, the war was the last straw. They insisted that China follow Japan's lead. And they had an important ally—Emperor Guangxu.

Guangxu had always been fascinated by Western technology. He had a collection of foreign-made clocks and gadgets. He was also the first Chinese leader to read the Bible and learn English.

After the war with Japan, Guangxu began pushing China toward modernization. In early 1898, he invited his people to send him appeals calling for reform. This in itself was a radical change. For centuries, only high-ranking officials had been allowed to address the emperor.

On June 11, 1898, Guangxu made his move. He launched the so-called "Hundred Days of Reform." Over the next three months, the emperor made sweeping changes in China's government. He fired corrupt officials and abolished useless government offices. He insisted that mandarins be tested on subjects other than Confucius. He ordered the military to modernize its training and equipment. He also set up the Western-style Beijing University and called for schools and colleges to be built around the country.

Cixi felt that Guangxu's reforms went too far. On September 21, troops loyal to Cixi took over the Forbidden City. A group of Cixi's eunuchs rushed into Guangxu's chamber and seized the emperor. By some accounts, the angry empress slapped her nephew with her fan and yelled at him.

Emperor Guangxu was placed under house arrest. Rumors that Cixi might kill him were greeted with anger from the foreign powers. If that was her plan, she changed it. But Guangxu would remain her prisoner for the rest of his life. She often kept him nearby as a

GUANGXU TRIED to reform China's government, but Cixi put a stop to his efforts.

kind of pet who followed her around. Cixi's eunuchs pretended that their emperor was not even there.

Guangxu's top aides were not as fortunate. Six of them were beheaded. They screamed curses at Cixi just before they died. Other reformers fled overseas. Eunuchs loyal to the emperor were beaten to death, strangled, or beheaded. Cixi's wrath even extended to a troupe of actors that the emperor liked. Its members narrowly escaped capture and death.

Cixi soon reversed most of Guangxu's reforms. Conservative members of the court relaxed. Cixi had made it clear that China's rulers would not change on their own. No doubt she felt that she had saved the Qing Dynasty. Instead, she sealed its fate.

CHAPTER 15

Terror in Beijing

Cixi takes a position on the WRONG SIDE OF HISTORY.

For DECADES, CIXI HAD TOLERATED reformers who believed China could learn from the West. Now she sided completely with the conservatives. More and more, she found herself swept up in their anti-foreign rage. One group in particular caught her attention.

In 1898, a loosely organized army of peasants began attacking churches and other symbols of foreign influence. They called themselves the Fists of Righteous Harmony. To foreigners, they would become known as the Boxers.

The Boxers found most of their members among the poor and desperate, especially in northern China, where there had been a terrible famine. According to the Boxers, their problems were all the fault of the foreigners and their Christian faith. One Boxer poem explained:

No rain comes from Heaven,
The earth is parched and dry.
And all because the churches
Have bottled up the sky.

In early 1900, a few Boxers met with the empress dowager herself. They insisted they had supernatural powers that would destroy the foreign devils. Some claimed to be able to set fire to a building just by staring at it. Others said that they could summon millions of "spirit soldiers" to their cause. The Boxers also insisted they had magic spells that protected them from bullets and swords. Somehow, they convinced the superstitious Cixi that their powers were real.

Given royal approval, the Boxers went on a rampage. In June, they invaded Beijing. A large force of Boxers swept into the capital city. Their chant began to fill the air: "Burn! Burn! Burn! Kill! Kill! Kill!" Chinese converts caught in the streets were massacred. Even people carrying foreign-made objects such as clocks or matches were killed. By nightfall, flames leaped from churches throughout the city.

BOXERS WITH THEIR enemies' heads on stakes. Cixi supported this desperate attempt to drive out foreigners, who were blamed for China's problems.

The alarmed Western diplomats retreated to their compound in Beijing and dug in. They telegraphed desperate messages to their home countries, asking for troops to put down the rebellion. Warships from the foreign powers immediately moved to seize Chinese coastal forts. An eight-nation alliance—made up of France, Russia, England, the United States, Germany, Italy, Japan, and Austria-Hungary—began putting together a force to invade China.

Cixi continued to support the Boxers. She dismissed advisers who did not agree with her and met with her remaining council to plan her strategy. Emperor Guangxu attended these meetings, a kind of ghostly presence who was widely ignored. The emperor begged his aunt not to declare war against the world. But a week after the crisis began, she did exactly that.

CHAPTER 16

Barbarians in the Forbidden City

The Boxers bring more SUFFERING TO CHINA.

ON JUNE 21, 1900, CIXI PUBLICLY DECLARED her support for the Boxers. "The foreigners have been aggressive towards us," she said. "[They have] infringed upon our territorial integrity [and] trampled our people under their feet. . . . They oppress our people and blaspheme our gods. The common people suffer greatly at their hands, and each one of them is vengeful. Thus it is that the brave followers of the Boxers have been burning churches and killing Christians."

With the empress dowager now publicly behind them, the Boxers grew bolder. They launched a series of attacks in several cities, with help from some Chinese officials. One provincial governor promised protection to the foreign missionaries and their families who lived nearby. When they came to him for shelter, he had all 44 men, women, and children slaughtered.

In Beijing, the Boxers surrounded the makeshift fort at the diplomatic offices, but they failed to break through. The offices were defended by an old cannon and several dozen naval troops. The poorly armed Boxers settled in for a two-month siege.

Some of the worst fighting took place at Beijing's Catholic cathedral, a short distance from the fort. Hundreds of foreigners there were trapped inside. They suffered almost constant attacks. Food and water ran out. People ate bugs and tree bark. Sick children wailed in the summer heat.

GERMAN-LED TROOPS INVADE the Summer Palace. Cixi was forced to flee for her life. This international force then took revenge for the Boxer Rebellion by looting her property.

On July 14, 50,000 soldiers from the eight-nation relief force stormed into Tianjin and seized the city from the Boxers. A month later, the force reached Beijing and freed the foreigners there. By then, 400 people had died at the cathedral, about half of them children. The Boxers and Cixi's troops fled, leaving guns, uniforms, and flags behind.

The relief force thirsted for revenge. Soldiers roamed through Beijing, looting whatever they could carry and killing anyone suspected of sympathizing with the Boxers. Many Chinese women threw themselves down wells rather than be captured by the "barbarians." "The Chinese think the end of the world has come," one observer wrote.

By this time, Cixi and the rest of the court had fled Beijing. The foreign troops came looking for them in the Forbidden City and at the Summer Palace. Finding no one, they looted both compounds. Foreign diplomats and soldiers mocked the absent empress by photographing themselves in her bedroom and garden. They held up trophies they had stolen for the cameras—necklaces, shoes, furs, and vases. Cixi's humiliation was complete.

Death of the
Pearl Concubine

RUMORS OF A COLD-BLOODED MURDER
followed Cixi into exile from Beijing. Just after the
Boxer Rebellion, the Pearl Concubine, Guangxu's
favorite, was found dead at the bottom of a well. Rumors
circulated that Cixi had ordered her eunuchs to kill
her. Supposedly, Cixi had flown into a rage because the
concubine had wanted Emperor Guangxu to stay in
Beijing and negotiate with the foreign powers.

Cixi's supporters defend her by pointing out that the
empress dowager had left days before the Pearl Concubine
died. Perhaps the concubine simply committed suicide, as
many other women did during the invasion. But that
raises another question: Why was the emperor's favorite
left behind to suffer at the hands of the foreign soldiers?

CHAPTER 17

Death of an Empress

A humbled Cixi MAKES HER PEACE.

RUMOR HAD IT THAT CIXI ESCAPED FROM Beijing disguised as a peasant woman. The story outraged the empress dowager, who was insulted by the suggestion.

Disguised or not, Cixi's pride was badly crushed by the flight from Beijing. The journey turned into a grim replay of the 1860 flight to Jehol. Riding on sedan chairs and carts, the imperial court wound its way 700 miles to Sian.

But Cixi was 65 years old, hardly a young concubine anymore. "I had a very hard time traveling in a sedan chair, from early morning before the sun rose, until dark," she later said. "It rained so much that some of the carriers ran away. Some of the mules died suddenly. It was very hot, and the rain was pouring down on our heads. . . . I cannot tell you how fatigued I was."

Cixi asked Li Hongzhang to negotiate with the foreign powers. China once again faced a humiliating peace. On September 7, 1901, all sides signed the "Boxer Protocols." Among other things, China had to destroy any forts along the coast, stop importing weapons for two years, and apologize for the uprising. China also had to pay a huge penalty to the foreign powers—about five years of income for the Qing government.

Cixi and Guangxu were allowed to remain in office, but they had little power. Foreign diplomats identified 12 Manchu princes as the rebellion's ringleaders. Under orders from the foreigners, Cixi had them executed, exiled, or imprisoned.

Outside the Forbidden City, China struggled to recover from the devastation of the rebellion. In less than two months of fighting, the Boxers had killed nearly 250 missionaries and more than 18,000 Chinese Christians. The foreign soldiers killed as many as 50,000 Chinese, many of them civilians who were suspected of sympathizing with the Boxers.

Empress Dowager Cixi's return to Beijing ended on a symbolic note. Both she and the emperor made the last leg of the journey by railroad. It was the first time that either had been on a train. Both were delighted by the experience.

The Beijing that Cixi entered on January 7, 1902, was different from the one she had left. The Forbidden City's palaces, libraries, and holiest temples had all been smashed and looted. Some buildings had been burned. Huge gaps appeared in walls where valuable objects had been pried loose. Fragments of broken porcelain, jade, ivory, and marble lay scattered all about.

THE ANCIENT CAPITAL of Beijing had been devastated. Much of the city was destroyed by the Boxers' riots and the violent response of the international forces.

Other things had changed as well. The Boxer Protocols called for face-to-face meetings between foreign diplomats and the royal family. For Cixi, it was a major change. But she seemed to adjust with grace. Her first invitations went out to the wives and children of diplomats. These were the very people that the Boxers had tried to kill two years before. But Cixi disarmed them with a tearful apology. She also charmed them by trying to speak English and by presenting them with her own artwork as gifts.

EMPRESS CIXI is tended by her servants in this photograph
taken five years before her death.

Every so often Cixi still showed her claws. She had a Chinese journalist beaten to death for criticizing her. And her treatment of Guangxu was often bizarrely cruel. At times she would invite him to dine with her. He had to kneel at the table where she was seated and eat from her hand.

The end of Cixi's long reign finally came in November 1908. Guangxu had been ill for years with liver disease and severe depression. On November 13, he slipped into a coma and was taken to the Pavilion of Peaceful Longevity to die. He held on for one more day before "ascending the Dragon to be a guest on high."

The Dragon was waiting for Cixi as well. Four years before, she had suffered a stroke that paralyzed the right side of her face. On the day of Guangxu's death, Cixi had a second stroke. Doctors tried to reassure her. But she realized that the end was near. On November 15, her health sank rapidly. That afternoon, China's empress dowager died.

Wicked?

After Cixi's death, the next ruler of the Chinese empire was five-year-old Puyi, a nephew of Emperor Guangxu. Puyi's reign was short. In 1912, reformers overthrew the Qing Dynasty and replaced it with a republic. The Chinese Empire had endured since the third century B.C. It had survived the fall of seven major dynasties. But it died along with the Qing.

Cixi has been called one of history's wickedest women. Her critics say that she ruthlessly clung to power and poisoned opponents who got in her way. They also claim that her conservative policies caused the deaths of thousands of people and destroyed the culture she was trying to preserve.

The more personal charges against Cixi are hard to prove. The Forbidden City was a secretive place, and there's not much evidence that Cixi poisoned her enemies. It's true that many people died at convenient times in Cixi's career. But in each case, there were signs that they died of natural causes. Even if they were poisoned, no one has been able to prove that Cixi was guilty.

Cixi's political failures are more obvious. She used her talents to hang onto power, not to use her power for the good of the people. She spent public money on her own luxuries when it was clearly needed elsewhere. She

EMPRESS CIXI POSES with the wives of foreign diplomats sometime after 1902. She spent her last years forced to cooperate with the Western powers she had tried so hard to expel from China.

remained short-sighted and rigid at a time when China needed fresh thinking and bold action. She ignored the wider world even as it was crashing in on her. All of these flaws cost her people dearly.

A leader is often measured by her legacy, and Cixi's legacy is a disaster. For China, the four decades after her death were marked by revolution, warlord rule, and civil war. The chaos did not spare Cixi even in the grave In 1928, Chinese Nationalist troops ransacked her rich tomb. The rings, pearls, and jade that had been buried with Cixi soon adorned the wives of China's warlords.

Chinese Communists seemed to put an end to China's turmoil in 1949 by winning control of the country. But the weary nation found that it had merely exchanged one tyrant for another. Communist leader Mao Tse-tung was just as cruel and destructive as the wickedest of emperors.

Of course, Cixi can't be held solely responsible for China's troubles. She had plenty of help from anti-foreign princes, corrupt politicians, and selfish eunuchs.

Most of all, she was forced into bad choices by the greed of foreign countries. They carved up China for their own gain and then blamed Cixi for the problems that followed.

Whatever her flaws, Cixi was a remarkable person. She was a woman who ruled in a man's world. Without her strong hand, China might have crumbled into chaos long before it did.

On the last day of her life, Cixi reportedly said, "Looking back upon the memories of these last fifty years, I perceive how calamities from within and aggression from without have come upon us in relentless succession, and that my life has never enjoyed a moment's respite from anxiety."

Perhaps under happier circumstances, Cixi might not have seemed wicked at all.

Timeline of Terror
1835

November 29, 1835: Cixi is born.

1851: Cixi becomes a royal concubine and enters the Forbidden City. The Taiping Rebellion begins.

1857: The Second Opium War begins against England and France.

August 22, 1861: Emperor Xianfeng dies.

June 1870: The Tianjin Massacre of Christians enrages the foreign powers.

April 9, 1881: Empress Dowager Cian dies.

March 1889: Cixi announces her retirement as regent for Emperor Guangxu.

June 1898: Emperor Guangxu launches the Hundred Days of Reform.

June–August 1900: The ill-fated Boxer Rebellion takes place. A foreign army invades Beijing, forcing Cixi to flee.

August 1842: The Chinese sign the Treaty of Nanjing after losing the First Opium War. It is the first of many treaties that rob China of land, money, and power.

April 27, 1856: Cixi gives birth to the son of Emperor Xianfeng. He will become Emperor Tongzhi.

October 1860: The British burn the Summer Palace.

July 1864: The Taiping Rebellion is crushed.

January 12, 1875: Emperor Tongzhi dies. Cixi replaces him with her nephew, who becomes Emperor Guangxu.

August 1884: The Chinese lose control of Indochina in a war with France.

September 1894: China loses control of Korea and Formosa after defeats in its war with Japan.

September 1898: Cixi arrests Guangxu and reverses most of his Western-style reforms.

November 15, 1908: Cixi dies one day after Emperor Guangxu dies.

1908

GLOSSARY

ancestor (AN-sess-tur) *noun* a relative who lived a long time ago

barbarian (bar-BAIR-ee-uhn) *noun* someone who is savage or uncivilized

barricade (BA-ruh-kade) *noun* a barrier to stop people from getting past a certain point

blaspheme (BLASS-feem) *verb* to say offensive things about a religion

billet (BIL-it) *noun* a chunky piece of wood

Buddhism (BOO-diz-uhm) *noun* a religion based on the teachings of Buddha and practiced mainly in eastern and central Asia

calligraphy (kuh-LIG-ruh-fee) *noun* the art of beautiful handwriting

chaotic (kay-OT-ik) *adjective* characterized by total confusion

civilization (siv-i-luh-ZAY-shuhn) *noun* an advanced stage of human organization, technology, and culture

concubine (KON-kyoo-bine) *noun* a woman who has been chosen to be one of a Chinese emperor's official mates, but whose social status is below that of a wife

Confucianism (kuhn-FYOO-shun-iz-uhm) *noun* a religion based on the teachings of Confucius, a Chinese philosopher who lived in ancient times

conservative (kuhn-SUR-vuh-tiv) *adjective* someone who opposes change and likes things to stay as they are or used to be

convert (KON-vert) *noun* a person who has changed his or her religion

corrupt (kuh-RUHPT) *verb* to make someone bad or dishonest

democracy (di-MOK-ruh-see) *noun* a country in which the people choose their leaders in elections

diplomat (DIP-luh-mat) *noun* a person who represents his or her country's government in a foreign country

123

elite (i-LEET) *noun* a group of people who have special advantages and privileges

embassy (EM-buh-see) *noun* the official place in a foreign country where an ambassador lives and works

emperor (EM-pur-ur) *noun* the male ruler of an empire

empress dowager (EM-press DOW-uh-jer) *noun* the title given to the mother of a Chinese emperor

eunuchs (YU-niks) *noun* men who could not have children and were servants to the Chinese imperial family

famine (FAM-uhn) *noun* a life-threatening lack of food

missionary (MISH-uh-ner-ee) *noun* someone who is sent by a religious group to another place to teach that group's faith

opium (OH-pee-um) *noun* an addictive drug that comes from the sap of the opium poppy

queue (KYU) *noun* a braid of hair, usually worn at the back of the head

reform (ri-FORM) *noun* a removal or correction of an abuse or wrong

regent (REE-jint) *noun* a person selected to act as head of state because the ruler is too young to rule or is absent or ill

seal (SEEL) *noun* a design pressed into wax and made into a stamp; it may be used to make a document official

sedan chair (si-DAN CHAYR) *noun* a portable chair that is carried by two men

shrine (SHRINE) *noun* a holy building that often contains sacred objects

stupefied (STOO-pi-fide) *adjective* astonished

succession (suhk-SESH-uhn) *noun* the order in which one person after another takes over a title or throne

Taoism (DOW-iz-im) *noun* a Chinese religious tradition that emphasizes compassion, moderation, humility, and simplicity

treachery (TRECH-uhr-ee) *noun* the act of turning against someone who trusted you

Find Out More

Here are some books and Web sites with more information about the Empress Dowager Cixi and her times.

BOOKS

Baldwin, Robert F. **Daily Life in Ancient and Modern Beijing (Cities Through Time)**. Minneapolis, Runestone Press, 1999. (64 pages) *Describes the customs, culture, history, and traditions of Beijing.*

Dramer, Kim. **People's Republic of China (Enchantment of the World, Second Series)**. New York, Children's Press, 2007. (144 pages) *Explores the history, land, people, and culture of China.*

Marx, Trish. **Elephants and Golden Thrones: Inside China's Forbidden City**. New York, Abrams Books for Young Readers, 2008. (48 pages) *A nicely illustrated look at the Forbidden City, China's seat of government during the Ming and Qing dynasties.*

Shane, C. J. (editor). **China (History of Nations)**. San Diego, Greenhaven Press, 2003. (208 pages) *An excellent overview of 4,000 years of Chinese history, from the earliest dynasties to modern times. Includes primary-source documents.*

WEB SITES

http://encarta.msn.com/encyclopedia_761576765/Boxer_Uprising.html
MSN Encarta's online encyclopedia article about the Boxer Rebellion.

http://www.dpm.org.cn/English/default.asp
This is the official Web site of Beijing's Palace Museum, which is housed in the Forbidden City and contains a wealth of information on the Ming and Qing dynasties.

http://www.museumca.org/exhibit/exhib_forbiddencity.html
The Oakland Museum of California's online guide to its exhibition Secret World of the Forbidden City: Splendors from China's Imperial Palace.

http://www.smithsonianmag.com/history-archaeology/da-cixi.html
An interesting online article on Cixi from Smithsonian *magazine.*

For Grolier subscribers:
http://go.grolier.com **searches:** Cixi; Opium Wars; Forbidden City; Qing Dynasty

AUTHOR'S NOTE AND BIBLIOGRAPHY

All historical figures have secrets. Cixi seems to have nothing but secrets. Even while she was alive, biographers struggled to penetrate the Forbidden City. They were only partly successful. Events about the end of Cixi's life are fairly well documented. Reliable information about her early life remains scarce.

There's no one biography that sums up Cixi. She is often painted as either a superhuman monster or as a nice woman who fell in with a bad crowd. The real Cixi lurks somewhere between these two extremes. Some of the most useful biographies are some of the oldest. Luckily, many of them can now be read online. Finding the real Cixi can be a challenge. But it's fun and well worth it.

Cameron, Nigel. **The Face of China As Seen by Photographers and Travelers: 1860–1912.** New York: Aperture Inc., 1978.

Der Ling, Princess. **Two Years in the Forbidden City.** New York: Dodd, Mead, and Co., 1931.

Gray, Jack. **Rebellions and Revolutions: China from the 1800s to 2000.** New York: Oxford University, 2002.

Headland, Isaac Taylor. **Court Life in China: The Capital, Its Officials and People.** New York: Fleming H. Revell Co., 1911.

Seagrave, Sterling. **Dragon Lady: The Life and Legend of the Last Empress of China.** New York: Alfred A. Knopf, 1992.

Sergeant, Philip W. **The Great Empress Dowager of China.** New York: Dodd, Mead & Co., 1911.

Spence, Jonathan D. **The Search for Modern China.** New York: Norton, 1990.

Varé, Daniele. **The Last Empress.** Garden City, NY: Doubleday, Doran & Co., 1936.

Warner, Marina. **The Dragon Empress: Life and Times of Tz'u-hsi, 1835–1908, Empress Dowager of China.** New York: Macmillan, 1972.

Special thanks once again to editors Tod Olson and Elizabeth Ward. They earned their money working on this book. Thanks to my wife Debra and our son, Zachary. I'd like to give special thanks to our newest son, Ben, who kept me company on so many late nights while I tried to understand Cixi.

—Sean Price